This Walker book belongs to:

_____

_____

_____

For Louisa

First published 1986 by Walker Books Ltd
87 Vauxhall Walk, London SE11 5HJ

This edition published 2016

2 4 6 8 10 9 7 5 3 1

© 1986 Shirley Hughes

The right of Shirley Hughes to be identified as author/illustrator of this work
has been asserted by her in accordance with the Copyright, Designs and Patents Act 1988

This book has been typeset in Plantin Light Educational

Printed in China

British Library Cataloguing in Publication Data:
a catalogue record for this book is available from the British Library

ISBN 978-1-4063-7278-6

www.walker.co.uk

THE NURSERY COLLECTION

ALL SHAPES AND SIZES

WALKER BOOKS
AND SUBSIDIARIES
LONDON • BOSTON • SYDNEY • AUCKLAND

Boxes have flat sides,
Balls are round.

High is far up in the sky,
Low is near the ground.

Some of us are rather short,
Some are tall.

Some pets are large,

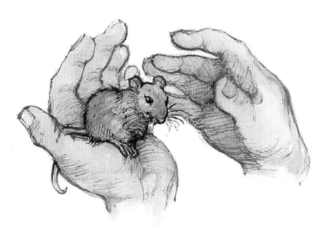

Some are small.

Our cat's very fat,
Next door's is thin.

Big Teddy's out,
Little Teddy's in.

Squeeze through narrow spaces,

Run through wide,

Climb up the ladder,

Slip down the slide.

Get behind to push,

Get in front to pull.

This
jar's
empty,

Now
it's
full.

Hats can be many sizes,

So can feet,

Children of all ages

playing in the street.

We can stand up very straight,

or we can bend.

Here's a beginning,

and this is the end!